BUILDING CONFIDENCE
IN THE
NEW CORRECTION OFFICER
115 TIPS AND STRATEGIES

SONYA DAVIS-ROBERTS

abbott press®

A DIVISION OF WRITER'S DIGEST

Building Confidence in the NEW Correction Officer
115 Tips and Strategies

Abbott Press books may be ordered through booksellers or by contacting:

Abbott Press
1663 Liberty Drive
Bloomington, IN 47403
www.abbottpress.com
Phone: 1-866-697-5310

ISBN: 978-1-4582-0757-9 (sc)
ISBN: 978-1-4582-0758-6 (e)

Library of Congress Control Number: 2012924090

Printed in the United States of America.

Abbott Press rev. date: 11/15/2013

Contents

INTRODUCTION

IF YOU ASK A CHILD what she wants to be when she grows up, she'll say a Doctor, a Teacher, a Lawyer or a Police Officer. Most children would not say a Correction Officer. Correction Officers are the unknown and non-glorified gate keepers of the criminal world, who are often and inaccurately portrayed on film as malicious, corrupt individuals. In fact, they're hard working professionals who sacrifice their families and themselves for a safer world. Correction Officers change lives. Their opinions are often respected and their lifestyles, often admired. More importantly, Correction Officers are the hidden heroes of law enforcement. They're always treated as second class behind the police, fire and sanitation departments. Yet, they do an equally dangerous job and play an equally important role in public safety. Correction Officers are the solid blue line that separates the criminals from the purity of society. As the military protects the freedoms of Americans, Correction Officers protects the public from those who no longer enjoy the privileges of freedom. A Correction Officer must be able to control not one inmate at a time, but an entire inmate population of twenty, fifty sometimes a hundred inmates on his confidence alone.

For a Correction Officer, confidence is everything. It is the equivalent of what a service revolver is to the Police Officer. Working as a Correction Officer is an exciting and rewarding job that requires you to wear many hats. From Guidance Counselor to Social Worker to Teacher, a Correction Officer is expected to do and know it all.

The goal of this book is to assist you in opening all of those portals with practical tips and sources of inspiration that can guide you through the difficult times ahead. This book will encourage you to remain confident in those moments when the rules fall short. Think of this book as your personal mentor. It can't replace the Training you will receive in the Academy, but it will help enhance your knowledge and put you in the driver's seat of every situation. The strategies presented in this book will help you deal with manipulative inmates who know the system. It will give you the tools that the Training Academy cannot and will not. These strategies will furthermore assist you in your decision making skills. They will help you maintain full control over your day and make you a better and happier officer. This book will help you enjoy your experience as a new Correction Officer and assist you in discovering the new authoritative person within.

PART ONE

GROWING THE OFFICER WITHIN

L AW ENFORCEMENT IS A VERY attractive job. The uniform, the shield, the gun; all feed our image of glorious heros. However, the glory is taken out of the hero when the hero feels vulnerability, caution, fear and has no gun. Working in an American jail robs the glory from the hero, but you are still a hero, no doubt.

When Correction Officers tour, you have no gun. But you do have thirty or more criminals staring at you for answers and leadership. The feelings of invincibility are immediately replaced by the reality of fear. To survive, you must use your mental skills and the confidence you've developed throughout your life. It takes a bold, maybe even foolish individual to step into a housing area filled with sadistic murders, rapists, drug dealers and pedophiles and make them listen to you with the confidence of authority. Yet, it happens everyday on this job. Your survival could boil down to your physical strength, but your success will be determined by your ability to think and outsmart savvy criminals and a complex department. Furthermore, many U.S. prisons have a large Female officer force. It is becoming more and more apparent that the average Correction Officer will not have the upper hand in Physical combat to control an aggressive male prison population. The reality is physical strength must be replaced by technology and mental ability if any correction department wants to survive. This leads to the average Correction Officer's own willingness to build him or herself up with confidence, knowledge, style and the simple common sense needed to be on top of their game.

An Officer can be effective in many ways, but take away any of the above attributes and you've lost the game. You've lost to the inmates, to your peers and to the department. Remember, your sole purpose in this game is to win. So, recognize and master these skills and develop into the officer you need to be to gain respect and have a long lasting successful Correction Officer career.

1 YOUR NEW OUTSIDE LIFE

Welcome to Corrections. It is one of the best jobs with the best benefits in New York City and any other city in the United States. The medical benefits are great and the pregnancy benefits are even better thanks to a large lawsuit in the early 1990's. But that's water under the bridge now. Welcome to a world of being comfortable. If you budget your money right, you can have a nice house, a decent car, a nice bank account and the right investments. You can travel the world and do whatever else you desire. You will lose friends and gain friends and find out who your real friends are. It's a great career if you just remember one rule...don't screw it up.

2 YOUR NEW INSIDE LIFE

Now, that you have a great outside life, take a look at your new inside life. First, forget everything you ever knew about a regular nine to five job. Your days will be long, your meal period short and every skill in your tool box will be used on a daily basis. Not only will you have to battle inmates on a daily basis, now you have to battle through aggressive co-workers and supervisors too. The rewarding part of it all will be your ability to laugh it off at the end of the tour, because when it's all said and done tomorrow's a new day.

3 EVERYDAY IS A NEW CHALLENGE

I remember when I first started the job. Just when I thought I've gotten through one situation on one day, the next day presented a new situation that baffled and stressed me out. Just when you've learned to handle one inmate with an issue, here comes another one with a whole new twist on things. Just when you've learned to handle a whole house, here comes a new supervisor who overrides everything you do and makes life difficult. Take it all in stride. When the supervisor leaves, make it clear to the inmates, they need you first. In most cases, most inmates just want someone to make an effort in assisting them. They don't want to be bothered with you no more than you want to be bothered with them. So, try to make the effort to do what you can and move on. They will too.

4 PRAY

This is not to scare you. It is to give you strength. As routine as this job is, there are moments it can turn dangerous in a heartbeat. So, when you step into the building of any jail say a little prayer for your safety and the safety of your co-workers. Many of the inmates in these systems are violent and mentally unstable and can without warning assault you, disable you or even kill you. Always, pray that you go home in the same condition in which you entered. You will get to know God, on this job. Because you will consult with him everyday. Believe me.

5 WHAT NOW?

Your day will start off with rushing to work. Even if you leave home early, something always goes wrong getting on the island. The outer fence alarm, a body in the water, a massive TSO or MAP. Once you get past fighting for a parking space, clearing the front of the Samuel Perry building, getting on the route bus and clearing the manometer at the jail's entrance and finally getting through another over stimulating roll call brief, you're already in a bad mood. This is just the beginning of your day, so try to stay positive. The attitude you develop here will dictate the rest of your day. So, no matter what your day was like getting to roll call, think of the end of roll call as the start of your day, not the moment you wake up.

6 RUSH, RUSH, RUSH

From this point on its rush, rush, rush. Everyone is rushing to relieve the officers from the last tour; the search is about to start. You need to get to your post, conduct your count, do your security check, count your keys, get a briefing from the officer on the last tour as to what you need to be aware of, count your floor cards, open your log book and pray that the search doesn't come to your area and disrupt the whole damned thing. Now, that you've finished everything, your day still consists of conducting your half hour tours, answering a slew of questions from inmates, civilians, other officers and supervisors. An hour and a half into your tour, you will be afforded a forty (40) minute lunch break, which might be disrupted by an alarm. When that's over, you will return to finish the last part of your day. If you're one of the lucky ones, you'll go home at the end of the day and unwind. If not, you'll never get a relief and never get a phone call which means you're stuck for another eight hour tour in the same housing area and your day starts all over again from the beginning. Through all of this, it is important to remember to stay positive and have a sense of humor. It's ok to laugh about how grimy the Captain was for not calling you and letting you know you were stuck. But think how angry you would've been if the Captain called and told you, you're stuck on the same post with the same inmates for eight more hours… That's why the Captain didn't call you.

7 ANTICIPATE YOUR ENVIRONMENT

The mistake many people make when first starting in Corrections is that they underestimate the true danger of their environment. Some new officers think because their lazy cousin Larry pulled it off without knowing anything, they can too. Big mistake. Cousin Larry probably never worked a jail or maybe he just got lucky. Don't depend on luck. Know what you're dealing with and take it seriously. Your actions, your decisions and your street savvy will be tested everyday. This is a jail environment filled with bad people most of who have chips on their shoulders. Many are defensive and some are willing to go to the extreme to prove their point especially to new officers. So, always anticipate your environment. Show that you are new to the job, but not the game. Go into every situation foreseeing the potential danger. Two inmates arguing can easily turn into an assault on staff or even an inmate death. Stay alert.

8 GET THE DROP ON THEM

This means do the little things first. Don't wait until something blows up in your face. Learn their names quickly to easily identify them from the beginning. The first few times you work a house, walk on the post with the floor cards. If an inmate tries to challenge you, look through the floor cards, match the picture with the inmate and address him by his full or first name. Give the impression that you've got his name and his game already. Now instruct the inmate to address you properly or simply back up. He will walk away or adjust his attitude. Inmates and other onlookers respect those who are professional and street smart at the same time.

9 LEARN THE TOOLS FOR SUCCESS

In this section we will learn about the tools for a successful career. However, we first have to define what is success on this job. Some officers say success is not having to write all day. Others think that not being written up at all is successful. Others think that being accepted by inmates or not having problems with inmates are forms of success, to each his own. Success to me was a combination of things that ultimately resulted in my retirement after twenty-one years without being (successfully) written up, without getting hurt or mangled and finding peace within myself for the foolishness I had to endure. Throughout my career, I followed a regiment of ingredients for success. They are as follows;

» Be Fair

» Be Firm

» Have a consistent approach

» Be Flexible when necessary

» Have a positive attitude

» Have a sense of humor

» Maintain your Integrity

» Get what I'm supposed to-like everybody else &

» Don't be corrupt, but if you are, be it all by yourself.

10 BE FAIR

The easiest way to get inmates to listen to you is to be fair. Always be fair. Many inmates feel that they were victims of an unfair arrest, unfair sentencing, an unfair shot at life, etcetera. Your presence alone is enough to make them feel victimized once again by an unfair set of circumstances. So, every decision you make about a dispute or anything will be under intense scrutiny by the inmate who thinks you are a part of some larger conspiracy. How you handle little situations is how you will be judged by them. So no matter what, be fair in your decisions concerning them and treat all of them the same. Treat them with dignity as you would want to be treated in the same situation.

11 BE FIRM

Being firm means maintaining a no nonsense tone. It means saying what you mean and meaning what you say. If you tell an inmate to do something, you expect it to be done. If he or she does not do it, address it. If it leads to a write up, write it. Don't give empty words that don't stick. Once an inmate figures out that you don't mean what you say, he'll embarrass you at the least convenient time like in the presence of your supervisors.

12 BE CONSISTENT

Having a consistent approach speaks for itself. You must stay the same day in and day out. If you don't allow something for one inmate, don't allow it for any inmate. If your specialty is a clean environment today, it should be your specialty everyday. Remain consistent so the inmates know what to expect. If you confuse them, they won't be consistent and you'll find yourself having to direct the same inmates about the same thing everyday. A lot of wasted energy.

13 BE FLEXABLE

Be consistent, but also be flexible. Being flexible does not mean changing with the wind each time you are challenged. Inmates do a lot of trying to change your mind. Know what you want done in a situation but keep in mind that situations can change day to day as well. If a clean environment is your thing and this one day you come in and an inmate couldn't clean his area because he is sick, don't insist the inmate get up and clean anyway. It's going to cause a problem. Learn to adjust to things as they happen. Make sure the inmate is seen by medical staff and explain to the inmate that you expect his area to be cleaned as soon as he can do it. Show that you are consistent and yet innovative when needed.

14 BE POSITIVE

Each day when you show up for work, you set the tone for that day. If you start off negative, your peers, the inmates and your supervisors will all pick up on it and act according to your attitude. A positive attitude will encourage another positive attitude. And likewise for a negative attitude. The department, by its very nature and clientele, is filled with negative people. This includes staff as well as inmates. Some were negative before they got the job and just continued their life's path. Others have allowed the job to make them negative. Either way, avoid them both, if you can. But as we all know, it takes hard work to stay positive on a job like this. Simply smiling doesn't cut it, not in this game. Try to keep your voice calm and remember to use positive sentences like, "I thought the directive was clear in this matter," as opposed to "This is that bullshit and I'm not having it." The latter, locks you into a counter action that you may or may not be able to back up. If you can't back it up, you'll grow frustrated. If you encounter a negative person, don't feed their fire or you'll find yourself just like them. They'll soon fade away from you because you don't have the conversation they're looking for. This also works with the inmate population. If an inmate is negative tell him to move on. A negative inmate will pull you into his world and have you fighting for your job, if you let him.

15 SENSE OF HUMOR

Inmates have a sick sense of humor sometimes. They'll find someone or something to compare you too no matter how good or bad you look. When I first got on the job I worked with an officer who had hair as red as Archie's. He looked like Opie from The Andy Griffith show. Apparently, I wasn't the only person who thought so. Whenever he arrived on post, the inmates whistled the opening song of the Andy Griffith show while he took the count. We pretended it didn't bother us, but inside I was laughing. Soon it was my time. An inmate got angry with me and joked that I had big teeth. This wasn't new. I grew up being teased about that and it doesn't bother me. So, I laughed with him. He looked confused and walked away. Whatever. I told a friend about it and she teased me forever. Learn to laugh at yourself even when you don't think it's very funny. Corrections can be a very cruel environment. If inmates find out something gets too you, they'll use it against you each and every time. If you can't handle strong or even cruel personal criticism, think twice about taking this job. It's not the place for insecure individuals.

16 GAINING YOUR INTEGRITY

In my experience the biggest part of my success was maintaining my integrity. As a newly appointed officer you are expected to change your lifestyle immediately. Many of you who come on the job are young and are about to jump head first into your first and maybe only full time job. If you were always a law abiding citizen, skip this section and go on to the next. No seriously. While I applaud you for having the good fortune of having a start before becoming a Correction Officer, many of your co-workers were not fortunate enough to have had that. So, while you can't understand why people have the philosophy that they do, don't try to figure it out. Just count your blessings. As for those of you who have lived a different lifestyle, please understand this. If you were used to partying with drug dealers, carrying illegal guns, shoplifting, abusing women, trying to run men over with cars, stalking people, sleeping with other people's husbands or wives, having children with known criminals or any of that craziness, stop it, right now! You are a law enforcement officer and you are expected to act, think and speak like one. Since my experience in the Investigation Division, I've learned that once you are off probation on this job, it's damned near impossible to fire you. But you can lose this job in a heartbeat over any of the above mentioned activities. All constitute Conduct Unbecoming of a peace officer others constitute fraternizing with inmates or ex-inmates and are definite job killers. I witnessed so many people lose their jobs over nonsense. Most of it is because as a new officer you're given Rules and Regulations, but most people won't look at them until they've already violated a rule and got caught. By that time, it's too late to explain yourself. For a person entrusted to enforce the law, your integrity is paramount.

17 WHAT IS INTEGRITY

Just because you are a good person does not mean you have integrity. Think of it this way; how many good people you know don't pay people back when they borrow money? I know a few. How many people you know who go to church but would pick up a wallet they found and take the money. Again, they are good people but lack some form of Integrity. Integrity can't be developed overnight. It takes years of training to fully understand and accomplish. The good news is anyone can gain their integrity with a lot of practice and living up to those expectations if they want.

Here's an example. One day I was off duty shopping in a supermarket near Riker's Island and went to pay for my food when a Correction Officer in uniform was in front of me on line purchasing several cases of beer. He himself appeared to be intoxicated. The cashier rang up the items but was clearly uncomfortable with the circumstance. The officer paid her and left the store and got into an official car with the alcohol, speeding away as he left. I was an officer, but felt that it was not my place to say anything. As most people I called myself minding my own business. Now, ask yourself this question. Which one of us lacked the integrity? Him? Me? Or both?…The answer is both.

He clearly lacked integrity because he compromised the uniform and he violated the public trust by doing so in an official capacity. I too lacked integrity at the time. I also let down the public trust. If this officer had gotten into an accident and God forbid killed someone, as an officer entrusted to uphold the law, I would have some blame in it. I had a duty to at the very least talk to him and tell him how his actions were perceived. At the very most, I should have reported him. The fact is most people would have taken the actions I took. But keep in mind,

Integrity is living up to the good, responsible officer we are all expected to be. It's doing the moral thing even when its unpopular. It's gaining the trust and respect of good people and good officers and dismissing the distrust of bad ones. It's being of moral consciousness. That's integrity.

18 MAINTAINING YOUR INTEGITY

Please understand that Integrity is a big thing with this job. If you don't have it, get it. And be careful not to let your frustrations with the job compromise it. Some people lose their integrity as they increase in rank. They lose it to be accepted by those in higher positions. They become part of peer groups and like high school teens, they are too immature to stand alone. Don't let this be you. Always do what's right over what's popular. A big step in being successful in the NYC Department of Corrections is gaining and maintaining your Integrity. The Training Academy will never deal with this subject, openly. They'll never tell you that some of its members including those in high ranks, lack integrity. They'll never address the matter so others don't fall into the trap. No. What they'll do is avoid the subject. The department feels it's not their job to teach you integrity, but they'll burn you when something goes wrong and use your unfortunate circumstances as a teaching tool.

19 GET WHAT YOU ARE SUPPOSED TO LIKE EVERY BODY ELSE

When I first joined Corrections I thought if I worked hard, I will be successful. I was wrong. The culture of this department does not lend credit to those who do a good job. You do a good job to save your backside when it's needed and to keep on top of everything. But it will not help you get what you are supposed to get. This department credits the savvy fighter. The only way you will get what you are supposed to get, i.e. a post, a good tour, training, appointed promotions, etc., etc., is to fight for them. This does not mean you are going to get everything you want but you will get what you are entitled too. Having seniority will not get you a post. Knowing how to intelligently demand that your seniority is a strong factor in the selection process, will. This is especially accurate during holidays. Most often the people who hang around the administration will get the holidays off whether they are entitled to it or not. Their *friend* will put them on a holiday post for that day, just to sneak them in. If you are not willing to sell your soul for favors, learn how to put up a good challenge. I made up my mind early in my career. I wasn't going to sell my soul for a favor and furthermore, my children were as entitled to have their mother for holidays as much as the children of the ass-kissers. Call it what you want, it worked for me.

20 IF YOU ARE GOING TO BE CORRUPT, DO IT ALONE

Sharing your corruption is one of the worst things you can do in this department. 90% of the downfall of most officers or members of the department in general, is doing their dirt in the presence of everyone and expecting everyone to back them up. If you like to do things dirty, (and I don't suggest that you do) you better do your dirt alone. If you don't, you run the risk of getting caught. I had a situation in my career in which a co-worker did something real shady with an inmate and threw the inmate back in the housing area. The issue came to light on my tour. Suddenly, I'm left holding the bag to explain why an inmate has injuries and why I took a post with an injured inmate and no explanation. Now, my actions and integrity are in question. Any indication that I was involved or covering up, would've been a stain on my record. Not! So, I did what my instincts told me to do...I had the inmate seen by the doctor and wrote according to what the inmate stated, how he got the injuries. This became an allegation. Not charges, but an allegation. The person became enraged that I didn't protect him. Although, if I could, I would've protected him. But not at my expense. The point is, don't do something wrong, walk away and expect other people to clean up your mess for you. Don't get other people involved in your dirt. Keep it in your hands and no one has to choose between protecting you or them. Because you will lose every time.

21 WHAT'S THE CONNECTION?

You might ask what does fighting for a post or acting alone have to do with growing the officer within? I will tell you. Learning how to be an effective peace officer requires you to be authoritative. You must take action when action is needed and to make the decisions that have to be made. Even if those decisions are unpopular and against the grain. Both of these steps relate to that. If you can't stand up and fight for your right to be treated fairly, how are you going to stand up and fight for anyone else you are in charge of protecting? Simultaneously, it takes heart to insist you are treated fairly. It's usually a difficult and stressful up-hill battle. The more you insist on fair treatment, the more likely it will become your reality. Fighting the noble cause is always helpful in developing your character and the new confident officer within.

PART TWO

BEHAVIRIORAL MANAGMENT 101 - IT'S NOT WHAT YOU THINK

THE CORRECTION TRAINING ACADEMY IS the spine of the department that teaches you the Alpha and the Omega of the job. You will learn how roll call is conducted, How to formally write your reports, about directives, rules and regulations, How to conduct sanitation, inmate laundry, religious services, what to do in case of a fire, and all of the things that makes a facility function in a clean, safe and law abiding environment. They'll explain to you, the recruit, how to write up an inmate in the event an inmate violates a rule. The Academy will also explain to you Interpersonal Communication that should help you prevent force. In the case of a Use of Force, the Academy will explain exactly what force to use to match the threat. The Academy solely focuses on how your actions are in tune with their liability. In plain English, the department only cares that they are not sued because of you. It's not the department's business how good you feel or how much you like your job or even how you came to the conclusion of doing something, as long as they don't have to hear about it. So far, that rationale has not saved them from being sued. In fact, it seems to have increased it. Because the department has not placed an emphasis on building integrity to its masses, these issues continue to rise and cost the city hundreds to millions of dollars to lawsuits each year.

22 THROWING YOU UNDER THE BUS

The DOC Training Academy is designed to teach new recruits to limit their thought process and think in a box. They don't want you being creative nor do they want you making decisions. They just want you to follow the rules. As bad as it sounds to a free thinking society, it's not always a bad thing. Some people lack common sense and the rules are the only thing that saves them from themselves. But when something out of the ordinary happens like an inmate in a wheelchair spreads blood all over himself just before he punches another inmate in the face twice and then stops and yells to you that he's HIV positive what are you going to do now? You need to get creative. The rules say you can't hose him down, or use chemical agents because he stopped his attack. There is no rule for this situation. Furthermore, you didn't act fast enough so you failed to protect the other inmate from attack and now you're subject to disciplinary action. You don't want to touch him and IPC is just not working. You're obligated to notify the Captain, but you are still the authority on the scene until the Captain arrives and you still have a legal obligation to act. All of the inmates are screaming for you to do something. This is the moment you feel the department has thrown you under the bus. If you do the wrong thing or fail to do anything, you may be written up, put on trial of terminated. Maybe even sued. Your action or lack of action will be used as a teaching tool to show your peers what not to do in that situation. Don't panic. You will prevail. Be creative and make an informed decision. Find the closest rule that applies and backs your decision. Justify everything you do and the department will have no other alternative, but to back you.

23 ITS ALL PSYCHOLOGICAL

Rules and Regulations say you can't use physical force to control an inmate's behavior. So, you have to find other ways to control his behavior. The best way to control an inmate's behavior and make him predictable each day is through what I call psychological warfare. An inmate has to know that if he breaks a rule the consequences are there. This doesn't mean writing him up all the time.

For one, you'll get tired of writing, even though this tool works. But to avoid having to take time out of your day, everyday to control the behavior of one inmate, you have to develop a style that deters inmates from giving you a hard time in the first place. Where is this in your Correction handbook?

24 STYLE

Your style is very important to your success as a Correction Officer. Understanding styles and its impact on behavior can help you become an effective officer who can gain the respect of the inmate population, your peers and your supervisors. There are many authoritative styles but only one truly fits into what we do because of the nature of our business. Maintaining control over defendants, many of whom are repeat offenders is very challenging. There is very little room for discussion. If you don't want mutiny on your hands, your style will have to be Authoritative. You have to have absolute power over the inmates. There is little opportunity for making suggestions although some inmates think it's their place to do so anyway. So, when you give an order it gets done and that's the way it is! There's only one problem, it usually doesn't work out that way. Most inmates are so used to not following rules that it won't matter to them if you have authority or not anyway. They're criminals and don't give a damn. That's why you need something else to motivate them besides your Authority and rules. So, think about ways to motivate inmates into doing what you need them to do. For most people, it's the threat of being written up that motivates them, but this can get old after a while for him and for you. Think about what will motivate you to comply in that situation and apply it. In my experience, I wouldn't take no for an answer. If I asked an inmate to do something, I explained to him I need this done. My tone told the inmate that I was going to get it done even if it meant stopping everything. And I did when I had too. Either this gets done or nobody moves. No phone, no services, nothing. Now a days, you can't stop a service. All the inmates have to do is complain to the nervous Captain or Deputy Warden and you'll get written up. So with this in mind, don't stop the services. Just run them like you are supposed to. Six (6) minutes on the phone for everybody (yes this rule still stands) use it if you have too. It motivates them to do the right thing everytime.

25 LEARNING TO READ INMATES

Learning to read inmates will come instinctively with practice. It means knowing what an inmate will do or how an inmate is going to react to something, ahead of time. Anticipating the problem prior to the problem allows you to have the upper hand in all situations. Have a plan of action before you enter any housing area. Always anticipate that in each area there is at least one inmate that is going to give you a hard time. Being prepared lessens stress and usually prevents a blow up leading to an unnecessary use of force. If you've heard through a co-worker that a particular inmate hates to be told certain things, make sure you have a plan of action for when you have to tell that inmate to do something and he refuses. Say to yourself, if he refuses to do _____, I'm going to do _____. Furthermore, don't just plan for him, plan for the consequences of your action. "If I order an inmate to clean up and it results in force, how can I justify force resulting from an order to clean up? If you anticipate and plan well, your orders will almost never end up in force. But if it does, be ready to link the order to the necessity and justification for enforcing that order with force. If you can't, you need another plan.

26 CONTROL FROM FIRST MOMENT

From the moment you step on post, take control. Give your first order of the day for the inmates to sit on their beds for the count. Say it loud, say it clear, and say it with confidence. All of the inmates will comply. If by chance one does not; single him out. Call him by name (you should have the cards with his picture) and order him to his bed. If he does not comply at that time. Get the floor plan (the diagram of beds and names) and start with bed number one. Find the inmate assigned to that bed and order him to the bed. Continue this until all of the inmates are on their proper beds. While this is a tedious task and you will at first be labeled an asshole by the inmates, it will work to your benefit in the long run. If inmates know you have an answer and willing to go the distance: no matter how tedious, they will comply just to shut you up. But don't worry about that. Before you get to bed number three the inmate that failed to comply, will suddenly realize you are not the one and will be the shining example on compliance just to keep you and the other inmates off his back.

27 PAT FRISK

The rule states that whenever an inmate leaves your area and enters your area, he is to be pat frisked. If an inmate leaves the housing area only once in a day, that inmate should have at least four pat frisks. One pat frisk, when he leaves your area. One, when he enters the area of destination. One, when he leaves the area of destination and lastly, when he re-enters your area. Unfortunately, sixty percent of your fellow officers are not in the habit of doing this. Yes, at least sixty percent. If you are one of those officers who pat frisk, you are a rare breed. The officers who fail to pat frisk, fail to understand its value to maintaining control over the population. Inmates need to know that you are not afraid or too lazy to pat frisk them. If you give that impression, they will play you. They will test you with little things; a pen, extra food, plastic gloves. Before you know it they're bringing in weapons, cell phones, drugs and anything else that can hurt you. Controlling contraband is the most important thing you will do each and every day. God forbid, the inmates riot and take over your institution. If they have a small amount of supplies, they will be very likely give up in a matter of hours. With large quantities of supplies the inmates can hold out and make impossible demands for weeks. God forbid if you are one of those hostages. You and your family would wish that the officers were not too lazy to pat frisk.

28 GIVE THE SPEECH

The speech is another form of style and behavior management. Most officers are too intimidated to give inmates the speech. However, letting inmates know what you expect from them is a sure way to cut down on problems. So, before you take inmates out to chow, to a program, to a service or when you first enter the housing area, run down a briefing of what you expect from them. Tell them that you expect them to be quiet in the corridor, to stop on the red line, to listen to your instructions. Explain the consequences if they don't follow the rules: written up or a privilege taken away. The speech tells inmates what to expect from you. At the same time, you will see their reactions and know which ones will be a problem right away.

29 ENFORCE THE RULES EVERY DAY

This is self-explanatory. Be consistent. The fastest way to get into a use of force is to be inconsistent. One day you enforce a rule. The next day, you don't. Two days later you are back to enforcing the rule with a vengeance. The inmates are only human. If they are unsure of what they can or cannot do, they'll do what they want or won't do anything. You will soon think they are playing you and a conflict will develop. So, try to be as consistent as possible. If something changes from day to day, explain why it's changed for that day. Not because you have too, but to make life easier for you.

30 LEAVE YOUR PRIDE AT THE DOOR

This is continued from what I just said about explaining things not because you have too but to make things easier for you. I always found that inmates are more cooperative when you treat them with dignity. I realized this when one day I had a funny experience. I was on a TSO at C-76 supervising a massive search. The searching officers were confiscating property from an inmate. I could see he was growing very agitated and arguing with the officers. To avoid force, I walked over. He explained that the property they were confiscating was allowed through the visit and he was entitled to keep them. I explained to him that his property was being confiscated because although it was allowed through the visit (as he claimed) the items were not permissible. I told him he got over in the visit but now we will have to put the items in his property. He already knew what I had explained to him. But not explaining it and letting him continue to hold on to his claim and grow strong in it, was just encouraging him. He calmed down and closed his mouth, thus avoiding force.

31 MAKE A DECISION

To be honest, the department does not encourage officers making decisions. Too many officers make irresponsible decisions and it has caught up with the rank, which is perceived to be very, very incompetent by the higher ranks. Unfortunately, it's the department's own lack of preparing competent staff that has led to the whole fiasco. But if you want to be one of the few confident and competent officers and you want the inmates to trust your authority, you have to show that you are capable of making sound decisions. If you have to call the Captain every time it's time to make a decision to do something, you're going to appear incompetent and have a hard time controlling your areas.

32 DEALING WITH THE MENTALLY ILL

For the moment let's go back to the inmate who has spread blood all over himself. Some of the tactics I mentioned earlier may help to alter his behavior from getting to that point. But if he is really a 730, the code for a mentally challenged inmate, very little will prevent such an action. In this circumstance, you must notify the area supervisor. Everything from this point on is all psychological. Physical force may control him, but it is clearly the wrong thing to do because of his lack of understanding. Try to calm him by letting him know you can help. Don't threaten to write him up. You'll agitate him. Speak calmly, but let him know you're not playing games. Ask him why he is doing what he's doing and explain that you will sincerely try to help him but only if he cleans himself up and calm down. At this point, you have to be real. Really try to help him. If you can't, explain that his demand was impossible, but if he has an alternative solution you are willing to listen. Also explain to him that you will not let him play you. If he does, you will never try to help him again. Meanwhile, notify medical staff and the captain. Make sure the inmate is secure. Also take precaution for staff and yourself to be able to get out of the way if you have too. Wait him out. He will eventually, let you help him or just comply. Explain to him that you and other officers have all of the time in the world. Tell him you're going home to take a hot bath and eat a nice dinner and if he complies he can go back to his housing area and do the same.

PART THREE

KNOWLEDGE

THERE IS NO SUCCESS AS a Correction Officer without knowledge. You can have style, you can have confidence but you will only get into trouble unless you have the knowledge to balance it out. Your style depends on how you present your knowledge. The officers who have confidence without true knowledge, always end up in trouble. Know it all's with no knowledge. True Confidence, the one you are seeking to gain from this book, will come only if you have the knowledge. So, what is the knowledge? It's the thing that helps you make the decisions we just talked about. You must read the rules and regulations, directives, operation orders and institutional orders and mix it with some form of common sense to gain good knowledge in Corrections. People respect people who are knowledgeable and burn those who are not.

33 RULES AND REGULATIONS

Knowledge is an important step to building up real confidence. Knowledge in Correction terms is not just knowing the rules, but also knowing the unwritten rules. Knowing what to do when there is nothing written to address it, like everything I've mentioned thus far. That's knowledge. When God created man and set forth instructions to guide man throughout his life he did it out of love. When the department set forth instructions to guide you throughout your career, it was done out of obligation. God has recognized that man is not perfect. God forgives us for our mistakes because he loves us. The department does not love you. You will not be forgiven for your mistakes. In fact, you mess up and you will be burned with everything they've got. If you're burned too much, you can lose your vacation days, your post, and your job. Know your rules and regulations.

34 KNOW YOUR RULES BUT DON'T READ THEM ON POST

Your little blue book of Rules and Regulations is your department bible. It will hurt you or save you depending on how well you apply it. So, use it wisely. But remember, you can't read them on post and there is a good reason for this. The department does not want the rules to end up in an inmate's possession. So keep it in your locker and read three rules a day before roll call for the first thirty or so days. Once you are somewhat familiar with what you are supposed to be doing, you will know how to justify your actions when you are caught off guard with something. For example; if you are caught off post and ordered to write a report, your report should automatically refer to your log book that says you notified the control room (and name of who you spoke to) of a need for a relief. Upon not having a relief, you should have signed off post and back on upon your return. Before leaving your post, always make an effort to get a relief and log the effort. Even if you have to leave before the relief arrives, you are backed up with the attempt.

35 IF YOU DON'T KNOW BE NICE

If you don't know your Rules and Regulations or if you don't know how to write yourself out of situations, be polite. It's as simple as that. Supervisors have a field day with officers who don't know their jobs and have bad attitudes on top of it. If you are this type, you will become a target and an easy one. But if you still have a lot to learn and have a positive attitude, Captains have a tendency to let a lot go based on the fact that you have a professional attitude.

36 NOT KNOWING RULES DOES NOT STOP THE CAPTAIN

Just because a Captain isn't knowledgeable (and many are not) that doesn't matter when they're dealing with an officer who can't follow rules. Always remember, a supervisor always has the upper hand even if they don't know what the hell they're talking about. Don't go toe to toe with one unless you have the blue bible to back you up and even then they still have the upper hand. Other supervisors (even the admin dep) will protect them because they are supervisors. Simply feeling morally right will get you nowhere. Their fellow captains will come to their rescue even when they are wrong. And don't hate, officers are the same way. They back other officers even when they are wrong. So, don't think because a captain doesn't know anything that they won't go all out to give you orders and write you up. Taking orders from captains who didn't know a damned thing, was my motivation to become one. I figured if the department can allow them to have authority and make decisions, why not?

37 RULES AND REGULATION LOOP HOLES

Earlier, I mentioned how knowing the rules and the unwritten rules can save you. But it's equally important to know if a rule has a loop-hole. Sometimes rules are written to prevent specific violations, yet are used in addition to other violations.

For example; if you are late, you may be written up with a rule specifically designed to prevent you from signing in a false time. This is called a loophole. Some rules have loopholes, most do not. If you're written up, look for a loophole in the rule. It may or may not assist your challenge. But keep in mind the best way to prevent a write up is to do the right thing in the first place. Knowledge when applied correctly, really is power.

38 ALLEGATIONS

If there's anything that an inmate can do to spin an officer, it's an allegation. Allegations send the department from the top down in a tailspin. Why? Because when an inmate makes an allegation, no matter how outrageous it is or sounds, the person he made the allegation about has the burden to prove their innocence. The inmate doesn't have to prove or even answer when the allegation is proven to be false. He can go on and on making false allegations that don't pan out and still there is usually no punishment to follow. I had a situation once when an inmate threatened to cut me across my face with a razor. As a woman protective of my looks, I didn't take the threat lightly. I did not hesitate to tell the inmate that any attempt to do that would immediately result in his own injury. I meant every word of it. I wanted to make it clear to him that an attempt to permanently injure me would result in his own extreme injury. The next day his lawyer called the Commissioner of the department and falsely implied that I worked a certain facility and had used previous force on him. The lawyer knew this was not true, but unethically pushed my name in the incident anyway. I was ordered to write a report about the incident and questioned for two days about my involvement. Of course, the allegation was false. Not only are some inmates liars, some of them have unscrupulous lawyers who do the same. If an inmate makes an allegation against you don't panic. Even if it looks like you are wrong. An allegation is his story; your report is your story. Make sure you explain yourself clearly and use the department's policies to prove your point.

39 USE OF FORCE

Use of force is the most volatile situation in the department. No matter how aggressive an inmate is, you as the officer have to be right in your decision to use force. If not, an inmate can sue the department and sue you personally if they are wrongfully injured. If you find yourself in a situation where force is unavoidable, notify your area supervisor. If on the other hand, you are in a situation where the Captain can't get to you fast enough and you have to make a decision. This is called spontaneous force. The department has already given you guidelines on what to do in case this happens. By all means, follow the directive. And whatever you do, be justified in your actions. In my experience I found that force, most of the time was avoidable. However, there are times things happen in an instant. But there are several good reasons to avoid force if you can.

1. Some inmates are HIV positive. Why use force and have to worry about your health afterwards? Was it worth it?

2. You can get hurt. If you try to grab an inmate who is aggressively swinging on you, you can get seriously injured. Who needs that?

3. You may be written up. These days the department is very pro inmate. Even if you are justified in your actions, they are looking to write you up for the temperature of the food because it got cold while you was using force. Do you really need that?

40 HARD TO DO YOUR JOB

I feel sorry for the Correction Officers of today. Inmates give you a hard time, sometimes the administration can give you a hard time. It's easy to feel discouraged. The good news is, you have this book. I retired when I did because the inmates realized that they were getting paid big bucks from false accusations and begin to make them all day long. I found myself spending 60% of my day, writing reports explaining why I hit an inmate or called an inmate a name. Only to find out, it was my day off or something. The inmates making the allegations are never punished for making false statements. The good news is, this book is here to help. Increasing your knowledge, your confidence and developing your style will discourage the inmates from giving you a hard time in the first place. An inmate will realize you're on duty and save his drama for a weaker opponent. Likewise, so will your supervisors. No one wants to contend with a savvy fighter. So do your job. Do it with confidence and you won't have to ever worry about false allegations or anyone giving you a hard time.

41 ENFORCE WITH CAUTION

There was a time in the past, I would never say what I am about to say in this section, but the reality is times have changed. But if you are not willing to go all the way, which is down to using force to get your point across, be careful. Ninety percent of the time, your words alone will make an inmate do what he is supposed too. But there is also, ten percent of the time in which an inmate needs more convincing. And it can happen at any moment, with any inmate. If an inmate knows you are afraid to use force, he will go out of his way to challenge you assault you or hurt you. Each person must make the decision on how far they are willing to go to control their area or any inmate. Simply telling an inmate whose been abusing the phone to get off can lead to a use of force. So, if telling an inmate to get off the phone is not worth force to you; proceed with extreme caution.

42 AVOIDING FORCE

Another way to avoid force, in many cases, is to simply address the inmate's needs. A lot of officers are too lazy to handle the things they are supposed to be addressing. This leads to inmate neglect. Once the inmate's frustration has boiled over and he's cursing and yelling, the chances of you having to use force have jumped to 100%. Address the inmate's problem and you can avoid force almost all of the time. Even a crab inmate understands that you are trying to help the situation. So, before force is a must, first try to find out what's the inmate's problem. If you can help the inmate, do so. If you cannot, tell the inmate the truth. Lying to an inmate may help you avoid them that day, but you will soon have to face an angry inmate who knows you lied to him and will not believe anything you have to say in the future. Tell the inmate the truth. He will accept it or he won't but you did your job.

43 DO YOUR JOB, FORCE OR NO FORCE

If despite all you do, you are faced with the possibility of force, immediately notify the Captain as the directive states. But don't fail to do what you are being paid to do and then evade the responsibility by calling the Captain. If you do this a Captain will have you writing from sun up to sun down. Your job is to provide the inmate with minimum standards; the captain's job is to ensure you are being efficient in your duties. Don't expect the captain to provide minimum standards. I had a situation once where an officer kept calling me for every little thing. The inmate refuses to clean, the inmate won't take down posters, and the inmate cursed her out; on and on. It became apparent that the officer wanted me to do her job. Needless to say, I kept her writing until she figured out what her duties were. If an inmate refuses to do something, find a way to motivate the inmate or write him up. Find a way to deal with the inmate without involving your captain. Earn your own respect and your own paycheck. This will help you in the long run and will help to prevent force in many other situations. If you try to get the captain to do your job, you will eventually gain a reputation of being incompetent and lazy. Eventually, you'll be written up so much you might have to fight for your job. Be wise, do your job.

44 WRITING USE OF FORCE REPORTS

If you use force, you have to write about it. That's the law. Don't get caught up in witnessing or using force and not reporting it. Next to using force, writing use of force reports is the second most volatile situation in the department. Learning how to write use of force reports is an area you will need to master before you even use force. My motto is "If you can't write, don't fight." That's all there is too it. The directive on writing use of force reports is self-explanatory. My only advice on the subject is don't ever put pen to paper to write a use of force report without knowing the injuries of the inmate(s) involved. This is simple protection of your report and your job. Know what you're dealing with before you write about it. If everyone is writing that they never touched an inmate, yet he has a broken nose, something stinks. Also, don't witnesses an inmate get stomped out and write in your report that nothing happened. If the inmate has a broken arm, you've just locked yourself into a false report. If you witness something and asked to report it, justify it. For example, if an inmate's arm was twisted while the cuffs were applied, there could be a possible injury in that area. So, write it. "The inmate was twisting as the cuffs were applied." That will explain why the inmate's arm is out of socket as opposed to trying to pretended nothing happened.

45 DON'T BLAME THE CAPTAIN

Don't blame the captain for pressuring you to submit your report. Rules and Regulations state that unless you are receiving medical treatment, you have to submit a report before you leave the facility. It's ok to ask the captain, certain questions like, how is the inmate doing? Or what injuries does the inmate have? Most will tell you. They still have to pressure you to submit the report, it's their job. But they are secretly hoping that you are smart enough to justify your actions, even though they can't tell you what to write. So, be smart. Your job is at stake.

46 KNOW WHAT YOU ARE DEALING WITH

Be careful of some of your peers. Some will mislead you. You will write that you were present during a Use of Force, but you witnessed no force. Meanwhile, the inmate has broken ribs. The next thing you know, you're going down with them and you never touched the inmate. Be careful which peers you take advice from. Many don't know how to save themselves; don't expect them to save you. If a peer is constantly being called to answer questions and have no charges pending, she's a good writer. If a peer is always being called down to Investigations or IG and is being charged, she's not a good writer.

47 KNOW YOUR CRAFT

Your craft is the way you apply rules, write reports and outsmart the inmates. Once you've learned your rules and regulations, it's time to learn how to apply them to your everyday duties. This isn't as easy as you think. The fact is even officers who know the rules and do their jobs still get written up. Knowing your craft means, having the confidence to deal with anyone or anything in the department with confidence. I once had an inmate who ran circles around every officer he encountered. I heard many stories about him, but I never worked with him until this one day. I could tell by the way he looked at me, he wanted to test me. But he was hesitant because he could tell I was not intimidated by him or his reputation. I knew my craft. I had no problem telling him 'no' and risking him acting up, because I already had in my mind that if it came to it, I would use and or authorize the use of force and write about it, no problem. I knew I could justify any action I had to take. He detected it. I never had a problem with him despite the fact he gave a lot of other Captains and Officers a hard time.

PART FOUR

CONFIDENCE

NOW THAT YOU HAVE DEVELOPED your style, gained the knowledge and mastered your craft you have entered a stage of applying what you know with confidence. The following tips will build your confidence and help you understand where you fit in within the department. Once you develop confidence you will never be intimidated or unsure of what to do again. Best of all you can work anywhere without feeling trapped or intimidated.

48 GAIN YOUR OWN AUTHORITY

Several years ago I was a Captain working the midnight tour. A new officer named Miss 'M" was working her very first tour in my area. I can see she was a little intimidated and unsure of what to do. Doing my tour, she came to me and explained that a particular inmate was being disrespectful causing the other inmates to join in. I told her to write him up. The 'A' officer, an officer who had five years on the job, told her instead of writing up the inmate, he would go speak to the inmate to tell him to stop. This is absolutely the wrong thing to do. When an inmate disrespects you, it is imperative that you, not someone else deal with him. If you depend on others to talk to inmates, the inmate will respect their authority, not yours. Gain your own authority. Deal with inmates, your way. I was glad when Miss 'M' decided it was better to write the inmate up and show him she was her own person. I'm proud to say Miss 'M' ended up being one of the most respected officers in the command and ended up developing a no nonsense style.

49 BE IN CONTROL BUT NOT CONTROLLING

I must admit there were times inmates felt I was being controlling as opposed to being in control. But that's because most male inmates are puzzled by female officers who know how to gain control of situations.

Where most of them came from, women can go to hell. This goes to say always be mindful of the line between being in control of a situation and over controlling. Your job is to ensure inmates are following the rules. This means you are in control. But if you go out of your way to make sure inmates can't do anything without your approval even to the point they have to wait until you come back to work to do something, you are being controlling. Don't think this doesn't happen. I've seen steady officers who restrict the inmates in an area from doing certain things until they return from their days off. Give me a break.

50 OFFICERS ARE THE BIGGEST GANG IN THE JAILS

I've heard this term and I really can't say that I like it. It takes away from our professional image when we embrace this remark. But in all reality in terms of control and willingness to use whatever force necessary to prevent power takeovers from the occupying gangs, yes have no fear, you are in the biggest, most powerful gang in the system. No matter how aggressive a population of inmates think they can get, the department has a use of force tool that can match them. If we have to bring out the smoke grenades and tanks, we will back them down.

51 PSYCHOLOGICAL WARFARE

As I mentioned before, this job is largely psychological. And although there must be a willingness to use force when it is absolutely necessary, almost all uses of force can be avoided through simple psychological warfare. The inmate population heavily depends on psychology not physical contact to intimidate officers and we must learn to do the same to keep them off balance. I once had and inmate who wore a Mohawk and was very, very intimidating to the staff. He never physically assaulted anyone, but whenever force was about to be used on him, he would strip his clothes and cover his body in feces to prevent the force and intimidate staff into getting what he wanted.

One day, he was in the intake pen and threatened to do just that if he was not housed in a medical dorm instead of the bing. Of course, no one wanted to touch him under these circumstances. So, I pretended to call the medical doctor while he listened. I pretended she gave the approval for him be housed in the medical dorm. Upon hearing this, he put his clothes on and allowed us to rear cuff him. Once he was under our control and in the corridor, we escorted him to the bing. Of course he was pissed off and threatened to flood the area. I took it as a warning and turned the water to his cell off until he calmed down. This could've easily been a use of force or an all-night situation. Instead, it worked just fine. I outsmarted him. This inmate and I went through several of these episodes before he realized I knew the game better than he did. He complimented me on knowing my craft on his way out of our custody. The point is, if you have too, use your instincts to outsmart the inmates when necessary. In the end, they will respect you.

52 DO YOUR JOB, EFFICEINTLY

The top reason for not surviving Corrections is failing to do your job. So many people in today's society simply don't do their job. Years ago you used to go into a store and ask a question. The employee would give you the right answer. If they didn't know the answer they would ask someone who did. Today, that practice has gone away. If you go into a store or any establishment and ask a question, you will most likely get the wrong answer. The employee is likely aware that they are giving you the wrong answer but they really don't care.

Unfortunately, this is common within the department too. Most people simply don't have the right answers or any answers. If an inmate asks you a question and you don't have the answer, look it up. If the inmate wants to know how to receive a service, you should know and if you don't, look it up. Asking the Captain should be your last resort. You are supposed to be a competent individual; after all you have a shield. Don't try to make it the Captain's job to know who the inmate can get razors from or who the Law Library Officer is. It's your job to know. Doing your job means knowing what to do and who to direct them to. Let's face it; inmates are the root of this business. You should be a walking information bank on how to direct them or inform them of department services. Instead, many officers don't know how to direct inmates because they are too busy placing the burden on the Captain. Don't show your incompetence by constantly asking the captain for information. Do your job. Have prior knowledge of information before an inmate can ask you. Knowing department policy, learning the function and names of each person in your facility is too your benefit. It's your job to be informative. You'll gain the respect of your peers, the supervisors and the silent admiration of the inmates.

53 SEEK LATERAL AND PROMOTIONAL OPPORTUNITIES

As your knowledge and style prevails, your confidence will peak. This is a time to follow your heart and seek vacancies in special units. Don't seek these positions before you have found the officer within and gained the knowledge we've discussed in part one. If you do, you will not fully understand the inner workings of the position and find yourself like a fish in a sea of sharks. Some staff in the special units are ruthless, conniving, and can really hurt your career if you don't know how they operate. On a better note, what you can learn in a special unit will follow you throughout your entire career and maybe your life. So, always look to move forward and up whenever possible.

54 DON'T BURN BRIDGES

These are the things the academy feel are too petty to teach, but they are so vital to your overall moral and professionalism. Don't burn bridges. This is very easy to do in this department especially because the posts and positions are highly competitive. Many people go out of their way to stab their co-worker in the back to get a post. And this is often done with the help of the Administration. As difficult as it may be, try not to burn bridges with your co-workers. Try to play by the rules and remain respectful of each other's feelings and needs. The administration doesn't care how you treat each other but you should. The person you are competing against today, could get promoted and be your supervisor, tomorrow.

55 MAKE IT A NOBLE PROFESSION

Be an example that others of all walks of life can look up too. Most inmates won't tell you, but many of them look up to us. They are constantly watching how we perform under pressure to see if we have the nobility and the right to give them orders. If an inmate doesn't respect you, he'll have a problem doing what you want him to do. I can't tell you how many inmates have approached me in the street and told me that they respected me and the way I handled myself. Others have praised the manner in which I spoke to them and helped them when they had no one else. It is always rewarding to me when an inmate tells me he has turned his life around and appreciate what was done for them during a dark time in their lives. Believe it or not, they are not all bad. Some have just gotten caught up and had bad breaks that could've happened to any one of us. Believe in the goodness of men. Don't let this job change that. Stay true to your belief that people are truly good inside and I believe you will be proud of what you do everyday.

PART FIVE

BE A TEAM PLAYER, BUT DON'T BE A FOOL

THE AVERAGE CORRECTION OFFICER CAN spend up to seventeen hours a day at work. So, it makes sense to try and build relationships with the people you spend most of your time with. Especially, in this job. It is beneficial to treat people who are the ones you depend on for safety and security, with respect. While I try to encourage you to be a team player, I do recognize there are some very negative people you will run across in this job. Be wary of them and do your best to build positive relationships with those who are positive like you. If you can, keep a cordial relationship with those who are hard to get along with as well. Not for their sake, but for your own peace of mind. A lot of them are filled with hate and are eating themselves alive. Try to get along, but don't be a fool. You're better than that.

56 FELLOW OFFICERS

Of all of the sections of my book, I find this one most difficult to talk about because as officers we should hold ourselves to a higher standard and be able to be mature in most situations; after all we carry guns and are charged with the duty to maintain order for inmates. It's disturbing when we can't be what we expect inmates to be. For the most part of your career, you will meet some wonderful, positive people. However, there are those who are extremely difficult to get along with and even harder to like. There is a saying in Corrections, "The inmates are not the problem the officers are." I agree with this statement somewhat. But God forbid a riot breaks out, you'll find out who the real problem is. If you don't get along with a fellow officer remember there are over a hundred people working in one place; not everyone is going to get along. If you find yourself in this situation, don't try to get everyone involved in the madness. Just do your job and hope that the person you don't get along with is mature enough to do theirs as well

57 IF THERE IS A PROBLEM

If it's a simple case of not getting along, don't burden the supervisor with it. It's your responsibility to get along with your peers, not theirs. Your supervisor is not the gate keeper to your social or professional life. Learn to work around that person without having to get the supervisor to make you two work it out. If just one of you is not mature enough to make it work, both of you will pay the price.

58 EEO ONLY IF NECESSARY

If by chance you and a co-worker don't get along, don't get Equal Employment Opportunity (EEO) involved if it's not an EEO issue. Too many people feel that anytime they don't get along with a co-worker it constitutes some form of violation of their rights. The fact is some people have not grown up. Some are immature, jealous and just plain mean. Many are raised with what most people would consider uncanny behavior. You cannot stop with simple words, a behavior that is more suitable for a doctor to deal with. So, try to stay away from them, if you can. If you can't and you feel bullied by someone on the job, first, speak to the person and try to mediate it yourself. If you feel that the situation is unchanged or has gotten worst, bring it to the attention of your Union Delegate. Sometimes they can help. If that doesn't work, bring it to a supervisor's attention and log it in your memo book of the date and time and the post each of you held. If it does not stop, bring it to the attention of your supervisor's supervisor and log it accordingly. If you still feel intimidated request mediation or a transfer to a better place. If you've taken all of the above steps and nothing was resolved, Now, you may have and EEO issue. You do not have to work in that type of (hostel) environment. And if you put up with it for months without a resolution, you deserved to be accommodated with an equal or better situation. Don't settle for worst. By all means, try to resolve the issue amongst yourselves before taking it outside of your rank. But be mindful that if the situation goes too far, both of you might end up transferred. Protect yourself by following the above steps.

59 BEEN THERE AND DONE THAT

When I was working a medical area, I was faced with a situation that I thought I would only hear about. An officer, who thought she was etched in stone in the place, disliked me. One day as I was relieving her it came out. She said she didn't like me because I'm always happy and smiling. Honestly, I thought she was crazy. For the life of me, I couldn't understand why my happiness or unhappiness bothered her or anyone for that matter. Then it occurred to me. She wasn't happy within herself and it caused her to lash out at those who appeared happy. What she didn't know was that I had serious problems of my own. But my issues were none of her business and I kept my issues at home. I soon realized not everyone is mature enough to think like that. Some people go through trauma and become angry on top of their sadness. It's human. But everyone needs to understand their unhappiness doesn't give them the right to make everyone and everything around them miserable. One day this officer grew too comfortable telling people off with no consequences. She became engrossed in a bad argument with another officer, who felt enough was enough. Soon this person was transferred out in a cloud of disgrace. She was embarrassed and looked ridiculous in the end. The sad part is, when she left, her so called friends who fed her madness everyday, clapped at her departure. I'm not ashamed to say, I clapped too.

60 WATCH THE COMPANY YOU KEEP

As you work with more and more officers, you will begin to get acquainted with co-workers. You will have some things in common with some and others...well; you will have a strong desire to vomit from the moment you see them. If you choose to build a friendship with some of them be careful of the company you keep. In Corrections, everyone will judge you by the company you keep. Be wary of the following types of officers you will encounter in your career. Some are good people but their bad habits can rub off on you.

61 THE INCOMPETENT OFFICER

Whatever you do in your career, please don't become this officer. This officer is one who shouldn't have been hired but for some reason usually survives years on the job before being fired. This Officer does not know their job, is constantly getting into trouble and is a danger to us all. He can seriously affect your safety and your job because he can't make decisions and allows the inmates to run the show for him. This Officer's actions will come back to bite another officer in the backside. Especially since your clientele are known for being violent and see all officers as their enemies. Do your best to know who they are and disassociate yourself from them at all cost. Don't give them up (it's the supervisor's job to figure out who they are), but don't protect them either. If you do, their next victim could be you.

62 THE I'M THE ONLY ONE WHO KNOWS WHAT I'M DOING OFFICER

This Officer is a good officer but she obviously does not trust the ability of her peers and is almost always doing everything all the time. There is no appreciation for this officer. Overwork yourself at your own risk.

63 THE DON'T GIVE A DAMNED OFFICER

This officer is not like the incompetent officer who truly does not know what he is doing. This officer knows some things but just doesn't give a damn. This officer is given a rule book but never reads it until he's in trouble (the incompetent officer won't read it, but will depend on others to tell him what to do). You know who they are. Taking long lunch hours, coming in late, sleeping on the job, cutting corners at everyone's risk and wonder why the Captain is always on their back. If you hang around this officer, you will develop the same type of lazy attitude.

64 THE KNOW IT ALL VETEREN

This officer, unlike the others has good intentions. This officer is filled with war stories about how they used to do it back in the day. The problem is this is not back in the day and if you do it like that now, you'll probably catch an indictment. So, don't get trapped into thinking you're going to get things done "Old School." Especially, if you don't know what you're doing. While you can learn some things from this officer, don't get caught up in their way of doing things especially if you don't have the experience or the know how to write it right or say it right when you get interrogated by Investigations; you might lose your job.

65 THE KNOW IT ALL NEW JACK

This officer wants to fit in so bad that they pretend they know what they're talking about. Usually this person has figured out that they have more common sense than a lot of people on the job so they think they know it all. The problem is, they lack the experience and usually find themselves having a problem with most fellow officers and Captains. If an officer has less than five years on the job, or has worked only one jail, and/ or worked mostly in limited inmate contact areas with under ten years on the job, you really shouldn't advise others on how to do this job. You have too much to learn.

66 THE READY TO RETIRE OFFICER

God Bless this officer for making it through, but stay out of their lane just the same. Many have a lazier-faire attitude and are resistant to changes and/or new ideas. If you make a suggestion about trying something new, you'll get the 'if eyes could kill' look. For an officer with a long career ahead of them, this type of attitude will be draining. These officers just want to come to work and go home until that last day. You have much more to look forward too at this time. Wish them well and move on.

67 PHYSICALLY ASSAULTIVE OFFICERS

This officer believe it or not, gets much love from the inmate population, peers and supervisors. This is the officer everyone thinks they can go too to resolve all of their problems with inmates. The problem is this officer is very often not a good writer and is constantly in the office of the Investigation Division trying to explain their actions. This officer is also always injured. They have uses of force, break an inmate up and then go out on comp while everyone around them who was involved in the force is left with the pressure to write the scenario of the force. When it's all over with, this officer usually feels used, while fighting for their job and has a long list of injuries to show for it.

68 BLOW IT UP QUEEN OR KING

This officer could easily be male or female but it's more often a female. This officer is a magician. Your day will be going fine until this officer comes into your area to pick up inmates or do a meal relief. The next thing you know this officer is yelling, cursing, the inmates are in an uproar and your calm day is now your worst nightmare. This is not the way to conduct yourself. If you do, you will find yourself always involved in a shouting match or just plain stressed out. Don't even let this officer in your area. If they want an inmate, bring the inmate out and take a short meal period.

69 THE GOSSIPER

Most people think this officer is usually a female, but don't rule out your male counterparts. I've worked with male and female inmates and in male and female facilities. I noticed the men (inmates and staff) gossiped as much as, if not more than the women. The gossiper officer is both common and popular. Because there is a lot of down time, most people end up gossiping to make the time pass. If you're the subject of gossip. Try to ignore it and try not to take it too personal. Most people don't know you and is just making things up. If you're exposed to gossip and you don't want to hear it. Make your way to the bathroom. When you exit the bathroom change the subject. Some of the other tricks are too look at your watch and pretend you're behind on your tour. If you don't want to appear rude, smile politely and don't comment. Most of what you hear won't be true anyway. The gossiper is a very dangerous officer. If the person likes gossiping that much they're probably gossiping with anyone who would listen including inmates. If you don't want inmates to know your spouse's name, how many children you have, where you went to school or what kind of car you drive, don't tell some of your co-workers.

70 THE CLOWN

During my career, I've worked in five different places. In each place, I've noticed one certain personality that appears to be everywhere in the department. It is the clown. The clown brings laughter to the job everyday. Many are a sheer pleasure to be around and can even make your work day seem shorter. The clown jokes about everything from the job, to music to life. You're laughing all day and at the end of the day, you feel like you got away with something. You can't believe you just got a day's pay for having fun. Most clowns are really funny. Their jokes are clean (mostly) and non-offensive and don't have hidden malice. Don't confuse this person with the alter side of this personality, the Joker.

71 THE JOKER

The Joker is the sinister side of the clown personality. Very often, you'll run across this person more so than the Clown. This person is almost always a male officer. The Joker can be funny, but unlike the clown who can make anyone laugh, the joker is not funny to everyone. The Joker is the Officer who jokes but the joke is always at the expense of someone's feelings. The Joker makes racial jokes, jokes about women or men; most of what they say is offensive and out of place. But they don't know any better. They use offensive language and very often incite and embarrass people around them. At the end of the day, someone gets offended and pissed-off. The Joker usually has hidden malice in his agenda. If you stay around this person too long, you'll end up in an argument.

72 THE POSITIVE OFFICER

In the mist of all of these personalities is the officer who maintains a realistic and positive view of the job and human potential in general. You may think they are rare, but as time goes on, you will see they are really not. Most of them remain in the background, drifting along doing their jobs quietly and efficiently. I know they're there. I've seen many of them throughout the course of my career. Most don't raise their voices, yet the inmate's listen. They take their counts, monitor the medication lines, keep a calm positive demeanor and unfortunately, they get very little recognition for a job well done. If you are fortunate enough to work with one of these officers, link onto them. Learn from them. You will soon see the success I'm talking about in this book.

73 YOU ARE NOT ALONE

The ratio of inmates to officer is usually 25 (or more) to 1. It's easy to feel alone when you step into an area and is expected to control all twenty something inmates. But constantly remind yourself that you are not alone. If things get out of hand, use your street instincts to hold the inmates at a distance. The directive in these cases have it right. Explain the consequences of their actions and use your IPC (Inter Personal Communication) skills. This serves the purpose of keeping the agitated party, distracted while you utilize your body alarm or

BUILDING CONFIDENCE In the
NEW CORRECTION OFFICER 115 tips and strategies

other methods to prevent an assault. But be comforted in knowing that assaults are usually rare and the support you receive from your peers, is plentiful.

74 THOSE ARE MY PEOPLES

During my career, I've observed some good things and bad things about staff who speak to inmates in their native language. I personally don't advise this unless the inmate really does not speak English and needs clarity and/or communication. But if the inmate speaks English and speaks to you in your native tongue and you correspond with that inmate back and forth in your native tongue, leaving your peers unsure of what you two are talking about, your cultural connection will be viewed as negative and exclusive of your fellow officer. You're asking for it if you make this your thing. Inmates of other cultures will not trust your authority (because they think you are being biased) and you will also lose the trust of your peers who'll somehow justify that you play the race and culture card.

75 A STORY TO TELL

Early in my career I encountered this type of situation. I was working as an 'A' Officer in my steady housing area and my 'B' Officer (a Hispanic male) and an inmate who I knew spoke English approached my 'B' Officer speaking in Spanish only. Throughout the day,

65

the two would converse in Spanish only. At some point, the inmate came and asked me for a razor. I explained to him that I was busy doing something and I will give it to him in a few minutes. The next thing I knew, the officer came into the 'A' station and was reaching into my razor box to give the inmate a razor. Meanwhile, they continued to converse in Spanish. The officer didn't realize it, but his actions offended me. The officer and I ended up in a disagreement about giving the inmate the razor at that time. The inmate knew what he was doing. He was using the officer to get what he wanted when he wanted it and I wasn't going for it. I ended up asking the officer to leave my post. The rest of that day and the next day, we didn't speak. On the second day, the officer and inmate had a disagreement that turned ugly. The captain was called and the inmate accused the officer of trying to extort him (suddenly all of this can now be said in English). The officer (via the Captain) wanted me to write a report supporting his version of events. I wouldn't and I couldn't. Because truthfully, I had no idea if the inmate was lying or telling the truth. If you speak in a language foreign to your fellow officer when dealing with inmates, don't be surprised if your partner can't back you up. If you make a special connection with inmates, you lose your connection with your co-workers. Furthermore, inmates have their own hidden agendas. Sometimes they have their own pressures to deal with. They could be using you. So, be careful. If your fellow officer can't understand what's going on between you and an inmate, it could play against you.

76 THIS GOES FOR EVERYONE

The above story is not limited to staff who communicate with inmates in their native languages. This is equally important for those officers who communicate with inmates in street slang or codes or other cultural connections. Since the recession, officers from all backgrounds and cultures have entered the department. Some people are not familiar with street slang. So, be careful about the way you communicate to inmates you think are your "peoples." It may take your partner too long to figure out you're not playing and you may be assaulted by then.

77 THE GREEDY BASTARDS

Every jail has those people who like overtime and those who feel that they are entitled to all of the overtime in the facility. The latter group, I classify as the *Greedy Bastards*. In today's world we are more and more exposed to the greed of Wall Street and the top 1% of the nation's population eating up 40% of the country's wealth. You'll find this same situation in the Department of Correction. Each jail has its 1%. One percent of those people who'll cut your throat to make the money. If you're like me (I hated overtime) you'll thank God for the Greedy Bastards. Because of them, I was able to walk out the door at the end of my tour most days. If you want overtime, volunteer and make it known to the supervisor that you want your money. Because if you don't, the greedy bastards will take it.

78 WATCH YOUR BACK

Shortly after I made captain I worked with a very popular female Warden who knew her stuff. She was smart and had a reputation for being an excellent manager. I spoke to her just as she was retiring because I felt I was unfairly passed up for a post. She told me something I'll never forget. She said the females on the job need to wake up. She said that when posts open, the women put in for posts hoping that they will be chosen based on their good records. The men, however, apply and then go into the Warden's Office everyday pleading for the post. As a manager, she felt that the men expressed the desires for the posts much more than the women. As you can imagine, I was not satisfied with this answer, because I felt my record should speak for itself. I shouldn't have to beg anyone if I'm doing a good job. I really felt betrayed because this same woman was also discriminated against for being a woman on numerous occasions. I felt for her to have been an intelligent woman, she shouldn't have fallen for it.

Let this example be a lesson to you (if you are a woman). Don't expect your record to speak for you on this job even if the decider is a woman who should know better. The egos on this job, despite rank are small and need pumping up. And the men are really good at inflating the supervisor's egos. Apparently, some people reward others who beg and make them feel in control of it all. Whatever. Understand that your co-workers are getting the edge anyway they know how. Never underestimate anyone, male or female. And always know that your competition takes no prisoners. If you want something put in for it, but also express to the decider that you are very interested in the post as well.

79 KISS-UPS, HOOK-UPS, F—UPS—THE INTRODUCTION

On every job you enter whether it's a private corporation or city service, you will see that each of these groups of people exists. There is always a co-worker who kisses up to the boss, bringing the boss coffee, sports tickets, lunch or anything that will win favor. Likewise, there's always someone who has a prior connection to someone in the company and is put in positions ahead of everyone else who's worked their asses off for it. And lastly, there is the classic f-up who despite all warning, manages to screw up time and time again. I mentioned them and while kiss-ups should be ignored, hook-ups should wait their turn and f—ups should be fired; very often they appear to be favored.

80 KISS UPS

Kiss ups as they are called, are those co-workers who will give you up for little or nothing. Most of them have no morals. They'll do anything for a 5 x 2 or 7 x 3 post even have sex with a supervisor. As you can see I'm not too fond of this category of officer. I've had my share of having to battle a couple of supervisors because they wanted to sneak their kiss ups into a post in which they had less time and experience. Fortunately for me, I knew my craft. I challenged one situation and got the tour I needed. Most of your co-workers who kiss up are insecure people who can't compete on a level playing field. Don't bother to dislike them; it's not worth your energy. Your job is to hold the supervisor making the decision accountable not your co-worker.

81 HOOK UPS

Hook-ups are people who usually have prior relationships or connections with someone in the agency. They're placed in positions of serious responsibility despite their lack of knowledge or experience. They get more respect than the kiss ass by far, but they are too loyal to the hook to be trusted by their peers. I always say, 'who you know gets you the job, what you know keeps you the job.' If you're a hook, make sure you follow the advice of this book and do your homework. Be the best hook up, money can buy. If people know that you will go out of your way to learn your position, you will eventually earn respect and make the person who put you there; proud.

82 F--UPS

F--ups are just what they sound like. They are many and common. The f-up is the person who is always cutting corners. They don't tour when they're supposed too, they're not accurate on the count or reports or anything else they're supposed to be and then can't understand why they are always on the a supervisor's shit list. This person just doesn't get it. They'll get written up and do the same thing again. The department has a hard time terminating these people. It usually takes years for these people to fight termination and many of them end up in sweet areas like a front desk, a filling office or being a Warden's driver. If they were in any other job, they would be fighting their cases from the upper corridor of a jail.

8 3 WHY SO BITTER?

The above descriptions are, what they are. There's nothing anyone can do about them except move on and keep a positive attitude. Unfortunately, the average officer who sees the Hook-up, Kiss-up and F--up get what appears to be favor while senior officers with experience are locked into working housing areas much of their careers, it's easy to become bitter toward the department. But you have to move on. Your business is to be the best you can be and not worry about who's getting what unless it affects you personally. Follow what I have laid out for you and keep a positive attitude; you won't have any problems getting to where you want to be in your career. You may not drive the Chief around but you will be in other prestigious areas. Personally, I feel I got everything I was entitled too in my career. Most of it was because it was my turn to get it. Other times, I had to file grievances, stand up to Personnel Captains, Admin. Deps., and one Commissioner Bernard Kerik, for H.I.D.T.A. training (he was very positive about it, in fact and sent me the very next time). In the end, I was true to myself, I stood up to those who thought they would get away with it but didn't and that is what counted for me.

84 ALLIES OVER ENEMIES—CULTURAL SURVIVAL 101

The culture of any agency is it's social and behavior patterns that has transcended generations and has assisted in it's survival. The Department of Correction has survived based on one sole aspect, it's necessity to secure and detain the inmate population of any city, state or region.

However, there does exist a social culture that has long assisted in the survival and success of it's workforce; it's social clicks. The social 'clicks' that exists amongst the workforce has dictated survival and acceleration of this group for decades. But, due to their exclusionary nature, social clicks are criticized and often frowned upon.

Members who join 'clicks' succeed by socializing and bonding mostly with other members they trust and those who are influential in their social circles. These are their allies.

In all areas of the dept., clicks compete for attention, favor and power. Furthermore, gaining information from your peer group and predicting political forecasts, post, unit openings and administration shake-ups gives you the upper hand over the competition. People in clicks move into more influential positions, faster than those who sail solo.

There is absolutely nothing wrong with clicks as long as they operate on a level playing field and the players don't become malicious toward each other. This sometimes happens. Competition can be brutal. If you choose to sail solo, keep abreast of the dept. political forecasts and stay in good graces with as many people as possible. You might catch a break or two when you really need it.

85 LEARN THE PLAYERS OF THE GAME

In every job, every city agency, there are people who are the eyes and ears of the boss. If you are new, I suggest you learn the players of the game before you make comments about someone. Never join in on conversations that are harsh unless you really know the people around you, especially in the locker rooms. They have ears. Save yourself from getting caught up in the everyday bullshit of the he said, she said.

86 NEPITISIM, CRONYISIM

Nepotism and Cronyism happens when influential people place family or friends in positions or posts mostly undeservingly. It often promotes conflict and the erosion of the moral fiber of an agency. This practice will likely exists in civilian or in-house posts. However, it's harder to saturate amongst the ranks because those positions and posts are achieved by tests and promotions. If it does take place, it's likely the person is qualified for the position. The best way to deal with it is to make sure you get what you are entitled too. Nothing else should matter.

87 OFFICER TO OFFICER

By the time I retired from the department, I was a Captain. But I was an officer for sixteen years and I've never forgotten what it was like. When I came along some officers talked about you behind you back and smiled in your face. Others didn't bother to smile; they just made it clear they didn't like you. Some were haters. Hating on you for being cute, hating on you for being in shape, hating on you for being ambitious, hating on you because you don't let them run you. Hating that you don't give them the time of day. Officer to Officer we don't have to like each other, but we have to trust each other. No matter how much you argue with each other, keep it clear in your mind that you have a duty and an obligation to protect each other when the time comes. Be supportive of each other and always be clear on who the real enemy is.

PART SIX

SUPERVISORS

WHEN YOU FIRST ENTER THE Training Academy, most of the people teaching your classes will be officers. You will catch a glance of a supervisor here or there. Most won't speak to you. When you get to the jail, things will be much more different. A supervisor does the roll call, a supervisor will tour your area three or more times a tour, a supervisor will instruct you on what they want from you on that day and hold you accountable for getting the business done. You will hear many different opinions about a supervisor, but your only business with them is to do what they need you to do. You don't have to like them or love them, but make sure you respect their authority and do your job and you won't have any problems.

88 GOOD CAPTAINS

Some Captains are good at what they do and unfortunately, some captains are not good at what they do. Most good captains were good officers. A good Captain is helpful, instructs well, tours with you, is consistent and is a good teacher when you need their advice or help. A good Captain is familiar with the rules and regulations, policy and procedures and if they don't know something they will try to get the answer and follow up with you. A good Captain is not afraid to serve infractions and should be able to help you write one if you are confused. A good captain will not steer you in the wrong direction. Don't confuse a good person with being a good captain. I knew many captains that were good people who were fun to be around, but they would get you burned in a minute. Not because they are malicious but they simply lack strategy and knowledge. Don't put your trust in someone simply because they're fun. Learn to separate the good person from the knowledgeable Captain and learn to put your trust where it is earned.

89 BAD CAPTAINS

Unfortunately, some of the most incompetent officers pass these promotional tests and become supervisors. Like I just pointed out, good officers make good captains. Simultaneously, bad officers make bad captains. A bad captain is the total opposite to what I said about good captains although some of them may have some of the above things going for them because they too have supervisors making things happen. But believe me; you will be able to tell a bad captain right away. They lack management maturity. It starts with the laziness. They hate to work, hate infractions even if an inmate curses the officer out; they rather allow the inmate to get away with it than have to do work. They don't think about the consequences of failing to back an officer up. The training academy does not teach new captains how to be good captains, just how to prevent their liability. So, as a new officer, you need to learn all you can about your post. If you don't care for one, maybe you'll be lucky and get a different one tomorrow. But the bad captain will eventually gravitate to you again. This is why you need knowledge and all of the things I mention in this book. A good officer can save themselves from a bad captain any day of the week.

90 GOOD OR BAD, DON'T TEST THE CAPTAIN

The last thing you want to do is provoke a strong opponent. My advice to you as a new officer or any officer is, don't test the captain unless they are seriously going out of their way to mess with you (and some supervisors will). Even if you know your bible (R&R) and the Captain does not, still leave them alone. Because when it's time to write you up, other captains will come to their rescue. You'll see that a supervisor, who doesn't know anything, suddenly knows everything. A supervisor can hurt your credibility and reputation if you don't know how to handle them. And realistically, 95% of officers can't! That's a fact. But if you must go toe to toe with a supervisor, make sure you know your craft. As I mentioned in an earlier part of the book when dealing with a supervisor, knowing your Rules and Regulations is not enough. You have to know how to write, how to apply the writing to the situation and how to trap the supervisor into such a tight space that he just wants to leave you alone. You have to find their failure to supervise the situation and include them in your defense. But remember, once you do this you may have other Captains and Assistant Deputy Wardens on your back. Just like if an inmate burned an officer, they will have officers on their backs.

The bottom line is if a supervisor orders you to do something (whether you agree with it or not) do it. Challenge them after it's done and only if necessary. Unfortunately, some supervisors tell you to do things just to f-- with you. The best thing to do is stay out of their way until you can't. If a supervisor gives you and unlawful order, bring it to the attention of a higher ranked supervisor. But this is so rare that it is unbelievable. In my entire twenty-one years of working, I've never witnessed a supervisor give nor have I ever received an unlawful order. Be very, very careful with this one. Unless you really were given an unlawful order, don't push this. You catch the right captain who challenges everything and you'll find yourself trying to explain to IG, what was unlawful about it. If you can't explain it, you will be written up for insubordination, false reports and unprofessional conduct. Those are real job killers too. It's not worth it.

91 THE NIGHTMARE SUPERVISOR

The nightmare supervisor is the supervisor who lacks so much in common sense that they are dangerous. The scary part is they have the authority to order you to do things that can get you hurt. For some reason, these supervisors go all the way to the top. It's crazy. There is nothing you can do. No one, especially other supervisors, will ever admit it on paper. Challenging a nightmare supervisor may establish boundaries between you two, but nothing else will ever become of it. You just have to live with them until they move on to a promotion, transfer or retirement.

92 THE TEACHERS

On the other hand, supervisors can be great teachers if you are willing to listen to the good ones. Just because a supervisor can go to your level and speak and act like an officer, does not mean that is a good supervisor. Always look at the supervisor's write-up history and successes at getting out of trouble. That is your main indicator if you have someone who will teach you right or not. I knew a supervisor once who was constantly getting into bad uses of forces. Every time you turned around, he was being brought up on charges. The ironic part of it all is that every time an officer got into a Use of Force, they would seek this supervisor out for writing advice. If someone can't get themselves out of a jam, what makes you think they can get you out of a jam? Seek out the good teachers and learn how to do things the right way.

93 RESPECT THE CHAIN OF COMMAND

One of the first things you learn in the Correction Academy is the Chain of Command. You will learn that your immediate supervisor is a Captain. A Captain's immediate supervisor is an Assistant Deputy Warden; then a Deputy Warden and so on and so forth. This is also true for inmates. You, the officer are the inmate's immediate supervisor. An inmate in your area with a problem is expected to go to you first. The same respect is given to your Captain. Any problem you have, discuss it with your immediate supervisor first. Give her the opportunity to resolve the problem without it going up the chain. If you go to your Captain and she ignores you or fails to resolve the issue, then you have every right to go over her head. If you go over your Captain's head without giving her the chance you're sending a clear message that you don't trust your Captain's judgment. In which case, you will cause tension. Respect the chain of command just as you would like the inmates to respect you.

94 KEEP GOOD RECORDS

As I explained earlier, do not provoke the Captain. But this rule goes for the Tour Commander, the Deputy Wardens, the Warden and or the department itself. But if you do, make sure you are in a no lose situation. Always keep good records. Times, dates, names, areas, the issue and who you addressed and their post. If it pertains to your area and duties, put it in the log book. If it pertains to you personally or how you feel and what you think, it goes in your memo book. If you think you are being unfairly targeted by someone, put what they ask you to do in the log book and your memo book. Your comparisons or opinions about it go in your memo book. Never put a personal thought in your log book. If you do, your opponent will use this lapse in judgment as a testament to your incompetence and unprofessionalism.

PART SEVEN

INMATES

I NMATES ARE THE BULK OF our business. In some cases, the average officer spends seven out of eight and half hours a day supervising, directing and counting the inmates. However, after using the bathroom several times, hanging on the 'A' post, calling different areas for services, contacting the captain for clarity on an issue, logging in the log book, taking extra time for your lunch break, going into the bubble for supplies, looking at floor cards and looking for blank reports, the average officer spends approximately four and a half hours a day with the inmate population. The bottom line is despite all efforts to spend as little time with them as possible, they are still unavoidable for much of your day. So, learn early in your career how to handle them. If you stay on the job for twenty years, you will most likely not be so lucky that you will never work with them. If you end up in a special unit, you're time is likely limited. As the saying goes, "Special unit today, an 'A' jail tomorrow.' Sometimes you work a special unit and then you get promoted and you have to go back to work the jails. Furthermore, if you work an inmate free work area you will be constantly reminded that if you won't play the game, you can be sent back into the jails at any time. If you learn to not be intimidated by inmates, the threats to send you back don't hold water.

95 WHOSE IN CHARGE?

When I first came into the department of Correction in January 1990 the officer had a lot more control and power over their areas. If an inmate disrupted an area, he was ordered to pack up and transferred out of the area, by the officer. But as time went on inmates began to file frivolous lawsuits that cost NYC millions of dollars a year. Now, inmates file million dollar lawsuits if you look at them too long. It's the e criminal's new 'get rich quick scam' at the city's expense.

It's a very unfortunate situation. By the time I left the job, inmates were ordering staff to escort them to the clinic on the midnight because they had a headache. I had an inmate demanding to be taken to a clinic in another dorm area; even though there was a clinic in the area he was housed. I guess I'm supposed to help him transport contraband now. When I refused, I was questioned as to why I refused to escort the inmate to a clinic outside his dorm. By the time this book is published, I cannot imagine what it's like. Anyone I've ever worked with will tell you I've didn't allow the inmates to intimidate me. Sure, I was afraid in some cases, but I didn't show it. My strategy has been the ingredients I've given you in this book. They worked for me. I hope they work for you.

96 WHOSE SPINNING WHO?

Learning how to deal with inmates' means not letting them spin you. You spin them. The example I gave was the example of an inmate trying to spin you. The reason he wants to go into another area that he's not supposed to be in is for several reasons.

a) He has contraband he needs to pass

b) He heard his friend from his neighborhood is in that housing area and he wants to see if he can find him.

c) He made a threat to an inmate in that area and wants to let the inmate know he can get to him anytime he wants too.

d) He's tired of being cooped up in one area and wants to stretch.

e) He wants to get contraband that is owed to him.

The possibilities are endless. If you drop the ball, you're going to look foolish when something goes wrong. And just because a higher up suggests you do the wrong thing, doesn't mean that they'll back you up when something goes wrong. If they didn't put it in writing, you lose. So, be careful. If an inmate tries to get you to let him into an unauthorized area, think of the reasons above. If you're ordered to break protocol by someone of a higher rank, log it into your log book that they ordered you too. Inmates don't care about you and sometimes neither does anyone else.

97 DISRESPECTFUL INMATES

Most inmates are capable of being disrespectful. If you give them the room, they will say or do something that will be overstepping their boundaries. Do yourself a favor, stop them in their tracks. Nip it in the bud from the start. If an inmate says something that's out of line, dismiss them from your presence, immediately! Especially, if you are a female. Let the inmate know that his disrespect will not be tolerated. If he wants to speak with you, he will learn to address you in a respectful manner.

98 WIN WITHOUT CONFRONTATION

This is the goal every day in every situation. As law enforcement in charge of enforcing a secure environment, we all just want the rules to be self-explanatory and at the end of the day, we can all go home with the understanding that the rule says this and everyone will follow and each day will be easy. Unfortunately, you work in an environment filled with rule breakers. If most of them could follow rules, they wouldn't be there. So, as the authority, you have to find creative ways to win each battle hopefully without confrontation. This usually requires planning ahead, especially when introducing a new rule. Always think to yourself, "If an inmate challenges this, I will say....If an inmate does that, I will do this." Once you've thought out a clear way to deal with any potential situation, you will likely win the situation without a confrontation. Remember the 5 P's. Prior, Planning and Preparation, Prevents, Problems. It works.

99 WINING THE CONFRONTATION

Working in a jail is very, very difficult. We can never lose sight of the unpredictable nature of the environment. Things can be calm one minute and violent in the next minute. With this in mind, there is always the possibility that an inmate despite your prior planning and consistent use of IPC skills can become disruptive, aggressive and violent. If an inmate becomes a problem and tries to be disruptive, explain to him that you will write him up. If he still doesn't comply and his behavior is now becoming a problem during a program; i.e. the feeding, recreation, medication, etc., then you need to stop everything. Yes, stop the services with the intention to run the services in small increment steps.

This means if for example inmates are on a medication line and one is becoming disruptive. Order him off the line (with intent to put him in the back of the line). If he does not leave the line let the inmate already at the window get his medication and then ask medical staff to stop the line until the issue is resolved. Give the inmates numbers (for their places on line) and then order (or housing areas) and inform them that medication will be resumed as soon as the problem inmate is removed or calmed. This puts the inmate on the spot. He knows that you've just made your problem (him), everyone else's problem. He will not be comfortable with that. Almost a hundred percent of the time, the inmate is going to stop his disruptive behavior. If he does not, order (or escort) the disruptive inmate to the intake where he will await to be served with an infraction. Then immediately notify your supervisor and presume the activities. Handle the inmates with confidence in every situation and you will win every confrontation, every time.

100 YOUR BUSINESS IS YOUR BUSINESS

The worst part of dealing with inmates is trying to keep your business, your business. Inmates are always looking for ways to get the upper hand on you. Its part of the psychological warfare we talked about in part four. So, it's important that you don't let them in on what you're thinking and planning. That ranges from your personal life to what they see you reading. Be careful what parts of your business you allow them to know about. To do this, you may have to limit the information you give to fellow officers as well. Some officers will talk your business in the presence of inmates. An inmate once told me if he wanted to know what kind of car I drive, he'll ask an officer.

PART EIGHT

THE HARDEST PART OF THIS JOB

BEING A CORRECTION OFFICER IS a sometimes difficult job, but it's also one of the easiest jobs, despite popular belief. Once you get the knack of this job, your days will become pretty much routine. In fact, you'll have days in which you will be bored to death. There is a saying amongst Correction Officers, "The hardest part of this job is getting there." This is true. But, sometimes you, the officer are faced with circumstances in which you will be forced to choose right from wrong no matter whom the players are. This, in no doubt, will be the hardest part of your job.

101 ADDRESSING A BAD USE OF FORCE

This is very, very hard to deal with whether you are a veteran officer or a new officer. Don't get involved in doing things that violate the use of force directive. If you happen to witness a bad use of force. God help you. Legally, I can't tell you what to do. Backing a bad use of force is a risk to your job. Not backing it, can cause you a lot of problems with co-workers. They'll feel like they can't trust you. I've had situations dealing with this. I've never had a problem letting co-workers know when I was uncomfortable with an issue. In return the bad ones didn't trust me. I felt it worked in my favor. I was never put on the spot to write a false report or to lie for someone. The best thing to do is stay far away from something that looks bad.

102 ADDRESSING THE BLUE WALL

Let's face it there is a blue wall. There are people who protect blue no matter how wrong it is. If you're comfortable with this, remember how outraged people get when police and wannabe police wrongfully kills unarmed black men. (Amadou Diallo, Patrick Dorsmen, Shawn Bell, Anthony Baez, Travon Martin). I bet you wonder how can some people protect the murder of innocent men. It's called the Blue Wall. Remember what I mentioned earlier in # 21. Some people don't have what it takes to protect the innocent from injustice, because they don't have what it takes to protect themselves from injustice. Rather than challenge it, it's easier to identify with it. The Blue Wall is protection for those too weak to stand alone. But if you are strong, you'll stop the violation before it happens. If you see a wrong is about to go down, step in and find a way to keep it on the right track. If you have a problem doing that, you are one of the weak ones. You are seriously, part of the problem. Nevertheless, if you find yourself in this situation, I suggest you do what's morally right. Anything else is unacceptable.

103 DEALING WITH RACISIM

Racism is still a subject that exist in today's society despite all efforts to eradicate it with laws, commissions and basic human expectations. The department is not immune to its existence. How racism complaints are handled is the true judge of how dedicated any agency is to its elimination. The Equal Employment Opportunity Commission (EEOC) is an agency put in place to prevent, discourage and punish those who engage in this type of behavior. You be the judge of how effective it is. If you observe any behavior or acts of racism, you should challenge it whether it applies to you or not. For this is the true judge of your own character. I'm a firm believer in equal rights. The more you expect to be treated equally, the more it will become *your* reality.

104 DEALING WITH EEO ISSUES

Let's face it; this is traditionally a male dominated job. With that said, there are men on this job who feel like this is no place for a woman. In fact, up until 2007, the practice of awarding posts based on gender was allowed. The directive entitled, 'Awarding male and female posts,' was coincidently discontinued after I filed a complaint against a Deputy Warden who openly told me "women don't belong on the job" and used that directive to shut me out of a security post. My case was unfounded, but ironically several weeks later, the directive was discontinued and no longer a policy. The rule was in place in 1990 when I came on the job and was in place until it was discontinued in 2007. This shows how it's never too late to challenge and change a wrong. Even if they will never admit it was wrong or give me or anyone else the credit for finally discontinuing it, the important thing is, a simple challenge to the awarding of a post was enough to stop such and open EEO violation. If you feel discriminated against, by all means file an EEO complaints. At the very least, question the decision. Just be mindful of the possibility it can be a lonely road. If you can't stand strong for what you believe in, don't bother to stand at all.

105 IF THE DEPT. IS SO SERIOUS, WHY IS DISCRIMINATION AND SEXUAL HARASSMENT STILL SO COMMON?

A true judge of how serious the department is in dealing with discrimination matters is to take a look at how common it still remains despite their policy to eradicate it. Another indicator is the department's reaction to discrimination complaints. I was an Investigator in the department for six years, a Captain for four and a half years and an EEO Counselor for six months. I can tell you the policy the way cases are viewed could be improved. Many discrimination investigations, especially Gender discrimination, require a substantial amount of evidence and witnesses. Evidence that is extremely difficult to gather, and witnesses that are sometimes too intimidated to come forward. Therefore, the department needs to find other, more reasonable ways for those who feel victimized to address their grievances.

The most effective way to eliminate discrimination is not to make it difficult to detect, but to make it extremely easy to delete. One way to lessen the number of complaints and violations is to treat it as serious as the department treats its UOF violations. If a ranking member is up for a promotion and has a pending Use of Force case, the department will not promote the individual until the case is closed and the charges (if any) are cleared up. This should be the case of a member who has a pending

EEO case as well. If the member is up for promotion, the promotion should not be effective until the case is closed and the charges cleared up. This should also be the case if one individual has too many complaints or found guilty of serious violations. They should be demoted, terminated or denied promotions. Then and only then would the department see a significant drop in complaints.

106 SEXUAL HARASSMENT

Again, this falls along the lines of EEO but it is very different and deserves a separate discussion. Most of the sexual harassment I witnessed deals with men and their mouths. No matter how much it is discussed, it just seems that a lot of men just don't get it. They simply feel like they can say and do anything they want and some, maybe due to their raising, just feel they don't have to speak respectfully in the company of women. My personal experiences where minor because when I felt I was being disrespected, I addressed it and it stopped. But most of what I witnessed surprisingly was women opening themselves up to men in supervisory positions to win favor, posts, days off or whatever else they were seeking. Some people are openly seeking relationships and everything is great until something goes wrong. Usually, by the time it becomes a complaint, someone got dumped.

107 THAT'S THAT BULLSHIT!

Get used to this line, it's a Correction Officer's answer to anything they can't see coming. An officer witnesses a bad use of force and doesn't give a report. Suddenly, everyone finds out there's a new operating camera in the area that caught everything on tape. The officer is asked to submit a report. The officer's response, "That's that bullshit!" The day went great. Roll call for the next tour just got on the way and your relief is coming soon. In less than twenty minutes, you'll be on the highway going home. A call comes in that your relief called in sick and your stuck for another eight hours. Your response, "That's that bullshit!" Get used to this one, you'll be saying it yourself before the month is out.

108 DON'T BE AFRAID TO STAND FOR WHAT YOU BELIVE IN, EVEN IN PURSUIT OF AN INMATE'S DIGNITY

Early in my career I had a situation that forced me to stand for what I believed in. I was the steady 1300 x 2130 meal relief officer in the Punitive Segregation area. I was conducting my feeding with the assistance of the two SPA's who were Hispanic and an inmate Kitchen worker who was half Black and half Hispanic. I noticed each cell I opened, the Hispanic inmates were given a lot of food and the Black or other inmates were being given a little bit of food. Inmate business, not my problem. One cell we opened a short African-American guy began complaining that he needed more food than he was given. I then ordered the Kitchen Worker to put more food on the guy's tray. The entire bing froze. The Worker pleaded for me not to make him give the guy food because the guy was on "the burn." I knew what he was talking about. If you were not Hispanic, you was on the burn. I informed the Worker that the inmate wasn't on *my* burn and *my* burn is the only one that counted. I told him to give the inmate more food or I'd fire him. The Worker finally came to his senses and gave the inmate more food.

I left work that day knowing I gained the respect of some and lost the respect of others. Whatever. Unless inmates are injuring each other, how they treat each other is none of our business. It's not up to you to make them get along. However, you have an obligation to ensure an inmate is provided fair treatment, especially during a service the department provides. This is why it is important to be able to stand up for your own fair treatment when necessary. I returned to work the next day to find I gained the respect of many of the inmates in that area of all cultures and backgrounds.

109 TRY NOT TO SABATAGE THE JOB

This is a hard one. I personally struggled with this one everyday. But the fact of the matter is most officers, once they realize the culture of the department they find it difficult not to speak negatively about the department. But to do this helps to erode the moral fiber of the job. Speaking badly about the department only breeds' dissent. So, if you want to feel good about where you work, try to keep the sabotage to a minimum. If you're that dissatisfied, take steps to change what you can or quit. But as long as you show up, don't challenge corruption and cash your checks, you are agreeing to the mission, the direction and the culture that develops.

110 THE MASS INCARCERATION OF BLACK MEN

As an African-American, I found one of the hardest parts of working in the penal system was the obvious high rate and systematic incarceration of black men. If you are Hispanic, the high rate of incarceration of Hispanic men maybe a factor for you to deal with and so on and so forth. Its hard being true to your oath of duties knowing the system plays a vital role in the criminalization of your people. I gained comfort in my position by keeping them informed of their rights and entitled services. It was the least I could do at the time. I made sure they had all of the avenues the system offered for them to prove their innocents. I recommended books and even had discussions about the struggle. But be careful not to fall for the *poor black man routine*. Brothers and Sisters will give you the business about not having the same opportunities you had. Don't let them make you feel guilty. You did your part being a productive citizen of society, it's not your fault that some of them did not. You can feel their pain but don't get played. As for those who may be innocent, leave it up to a jury to decide.

PART NINE

THE TWO N WORDS

111 DO NOT USE THE N-WORD RACIAL SLUR

As an African-American I felt the need to address the common, slang usage of the N-word. I will only say it's a racial slur in which was originally used derogatorily towards African-Americans and is very, very offensive. Because of the large portion of African-Americans that populate American jail systems, many who are ignorant to the damage the word has done to the African-American segment of our society; this word is used throughout jail systems in the form of a cool slang word. I've personally witnessed officers, black, white, hispanic, even chinese, calling each other the N-word. As an officer don't offend someone by using this word and mistakenly thinking that you are cool or down or just fitting in. You are a professional. If you don't want to be written up for conduct unbecoming or unprofessional behavior, don't let yourself go there. You can't do what the inmates do, nor should you want to. Just because many of them wear their ignorance as proudly as we wear our shields, does not mean its ok for you, the professional, to do the same.

112 THE OTHER N-WORD

There is one word throughout the entire prison system in America that has the potential to set a whole population of inmates off. The word is 'NO.' I bet you thought it was something else. This simple word has started riots. In my entire career, I've never met an inmate that can't go from all smiles to a full fledge riot machine over this one word. Simply put, they don't like that word. Never tell an inmate he can't have something unless you are fully prepared to feel his wrath. This is real.

PART TEN

THE TWO DISAPPEARING 'P'S

113 PROFESSIONALISIM

So many people on this job lack professionalism for the reasons mentioned earlier but there is also a certain dark element about the department that has to be able to get down and dirty to maintain control of a potentially violent criminal clientele. It's called force. And while people may complain about that, deep inside their hearts they know that society is safer because of the dept's willingness to use force when things get out of hand. This sometimes seeps into the psyche of the members and produce a very angry, destructive person who lacks respect for everyone around them. Professionalism is vastly disappearing from the department. People say anything, do anything. Nothing is off limits when they're angry. Over the years, I've witnesses staff tell other members things that should never be said in a professional setting. Instead of higher ranks. handling it in a proper manner, it's usually swept under the rug only to grow bigger on another day. Unprofessionalism in the department is from the top down, not the bottom up. Until the department learns how to prevent, address and punish unprofessional flare ups, there will always be an unprofessional element. over the department that lends credence to the reputation that DOC is filled with unprofessional staff.

114 PATRIOTISIM

Be Patriotic. I know some people struggle with being patriotic for their own personal reasons, but if you know what I know, you need to keep it to yourself. It is important to be patriotic on this job, especially in the performance of your duties. No matter how you feel off the job make sure you are loyal to the United States of America on the job. The City Charter and the qualifications for being eligible to be a Correction Officer or any law enforcement officer, is that you will uphold, protect and enforce the constitution and laws of the United States. You took an oath of office. Make sure you abide by it.

115 YOUR MISSION

Throughout this book I've pointed out the many ways DOC will hold you, the new officer accountable for your actions. But DOC must be held accountable as well. The NYCDOC and many other American prisons have failed to rehabilitate their prison populations. Presently, America incarcerate and reincarcerate black and brown people at rates higher than some countries' populations. The mass incarceration of black men is systemic and profitable, and serves to criminalize black men and black people.

Unfortunately, black men have played into this system. Through music they define themselves as drug dealers, pimps, gun slingers and niggers. Their sensationalization of these images has ironically influenced the popular culture of all American youth and social media worldwide. This is why black people are artistically admired and yet socially despised. In retrospect, America's mission to enslave, control and despise Black and Brown youth has reached the picket white fences of America's elite.

America and Americans must police it's prisons and force them to honor their mission statements to rehabilitate it's prisoners and create safer societies for all people. As new officers, you are the future decision makers. Think about how mass rehabilitation can positively impact our society. Your invested interest in your new career must include strong cries for rehabilitation programs, jobs, skills and housing for those released. You must reduce recidivism. If not, these men will be released into a world you, I and all of our loved ones live in with the negatives of a non-compassionate system. As you move up the ranks of this job remember this thought, "The society you save in here, will positively impact the society you live in out there."

Thank you for purchasing this book. I hope what you've read helps you through your new career. The goal of this book is to enhance your training and offer you a method of surviving, succeeding and building your confidence in the Correction experience. This book will not replace your Academy training. It is not a guarantee that you won't get hurt, written up or sued. It is for advice only. The Author is not responsible for anything that occurs without her knowledge or even outside of her control. If the methods suggested in this book do not work, try other methods that best suit the situation. Be your own student and your own teacher. The methods outlined helped me to have a long, successful career with the department and I wanted to pass it on to others.

Lastly, as you learn IPC (Interpersonal Communication), remember to enhance it with Integrity, Professionalism and Confidence.

Furthermore, always remember to stay safe, stay happy and good luck in your new career. Your fellow Officer and Captain,

Sonya Davis-Roberts

ACKNOWLEDGEMENTS

I'd like to give a special thanks to my family. My parents Charlie and Mildred and to my brother Vernon and to my brother Alvin.

To my husband, Tony and children, Aliyah and Omari. Love you guys.

To the whole Kester and Martha Mitchell family, who expected nothing but good things from all of us.

To my cousins Barry (Gully Gee) and Sue for your support in hard times.

To everyone on the job who gave me lasting advice, training, good laughs and knowledge that will last a lifetime.

GMDC
CO Kevin Johnson, CO Villa, CO Smith, CO Tillman, CO Cheryl Edwards, CO Austin, CO Janet Greer.

EHPW
CO Roslyn Spigner (T.T.B.O.D.), CO Yvonne Allison, CO Nadia Harris.

<u>Investigations Crew</u> - Deputy Director Andre Suite (An intelligent frat brother who taught me to see myself without limitations), Inv. Supervisor Robert Fernandez. Investigators, D. Issac, R. Stridiron, D. Eurie, J. Westbrook (cigars but no pork), J. Hartley, B. Ornes, K. McNally, D. Brown, T. Jenkins, Capt. McKenzie (There goes that news man again ☺), Inv. Clark.

<u>Captain Crew</u> – We grew together and learned how to lead, together.

Capt. /ADW. Michelle Hallett, Capt. /ADW Demetria Gives, Capt. /ADW Robin Collins, Capt. Vanessa Womak, and Capt. K. Jacobs.

ABOUT THE AUTHOR

Sonya Davis—Roberts began her career as a Correction Officer in January 1990. She was assigned to the George Motchan Detention Center (C-73). In 1992 she was transferred to the West Facility and worked there until she was appointed as an Investigator in the Investigation Division. She worked as an Investigator for six years as the Executive Assistant to the Deputy Director and in the Sick Leave Unit and as an Absconder. She worked as an officer in the Elmhurst Hospital Prison Ward before her promotion to Captain in 2006. She was assigned to the North Infirmary Command until she retired in November 2010. She began writing shortly after her retirement. Today she is an Author and Screenwriter.